To all those people who over the years have taken money or drinks from me after humiliating me on the golf course and to the very *very* few who haven't

Published in the United Kingdom in 2011 by
Portico Books
10 Southcombe Street
London
W14 0RA

An imprint of Anova Books Company Ltd

ISBN 978-1-907554-1-86

A CIP catalogue record for this book is available from the British Library.

10 9 8 7 6 5 4 3 2 1

Printed and bound by Everbest Printing Co Ltd, China

This book can be ordered direct from the publisher at
www.anovabooks.com

MAC'S TEE TIME

Stan McMurtry **mac**
Edited by Mark Bryant

PORTICO

INTRODUCTION

Some time ago I was asked by the sports editor of the *Daily Mail* to devise a golf cartoon that readers could participate in and which would appear once a week in the paper.

I came up with the idea that I would draw a cartoon situation featuring golfers and then invite readers to send in a suitably funny caption. The prize for the lucky winner each week was three dozen personalised Wilson Staff golf balls and the cartoon would be printed the following week complete with it's new caption.

At first there were only a few entries but after the competition had been running for a few weeks I soon became snowed under by cards. Some of them funny, some extremely corny and some just a bit too rude to print.

Judging the one-liners was very time consuming but I did look at every one that was sent in. After all, if the reader had taken the trouble to think up a caption, write it down, put a stamp on a card *and* post it, then I felt it should be read and considered.

There were a few angry letters from readers who thought their captions were far superior to the ones that I had chosen, obviously everyone at the pub had told them so. One crafty beggar even sent me a ten pound note hoping it would pave the way to him winning 36 shiny new golf balls with his name printed on them. It didn't and I sent him his bribe back (I bet he cheats on the golf course too!).

Anyway, here is a selection of the winning cartoons that were funnier enough to make it into the paper. I hope you'll like them.

MAC

1 July 1999

'Don't worry, the snake's a mamba of the club!'

15 July 1999

'Tell me, Mavis, is this your first sudden-death play-off?'

5 August 1999

'He used to work for Dynorod until he retired!'

20 August 1999

'So you're the Birdie Man of Alcatraz.'

2 September 1999

'Not even his ball ... some poor devil's pom-pom hat.'

9 September 1999

'Brace yourself, lad, this may sting a little.'

17 September 1999

'Poor Braithwaite, batteries flat, been there three days.'

23 September 1999

'Things can't get worse. Shipwrecked with
a homosexual fanatical golfer.'

30 September 1999

'I only mentioned I needed a new head cover.'

7 October 1999

'He ran off with the Handicap Committee chairman's wife.'

21 October 1999

'I've warned him before about parking in the captain's space.'

28 October 1999

'He thought the vicar said "Let us play"!'

11 November 1999

'Nice of you to ask but please, play through!'

18 November 1999

'I've heard of a sudden-death play-off, but this is ridiculous.'

10 December 1999

'This, son, for a pterodactyl three at the 18th.'

21 January 2000

'Perfection! Nicklaus' brain, Monty's body, the bolts
from Tiger's trolley!'

4 February 2000

'OK, on the count of three – we pivot!'

11 February 2000

'This must be the Golf Stream!'

17 March 2000

'I've got a terrible feeling that if he strikes that well, Cain and Abel will never be begat.'

31 March 2000

'Didn't you rake the sand at the last bunker?'

21 April 2000

'Coo! 275 yards and missed the water!'

28 April 2000

'That's the last time we play golf with Paul Daniels!'

5 May 2000

'I see the ladies' showers aren't working again.'

12 May 2000

' "Won prizes for my greens", it said on his job application.'

19 May 2000

'That was seven years ago – he's been supplementing his pension ever since.'

26 May 2000

'His best trick is where he feeds all the members with five
finger rolls and a tin of sardines.'

2 June 2000

'I knew you wouldn't miss our weekly game, Fred.'

9 June 2000

'If that's a gimme, I'm down for 3,947.'

23 June 2000

'Do you recall saying: "God knows where that went"?'

14 July 2000

'You will think you have scored a hole-in-one.
I'll be waiting at the bar.'

21 July 2000

'Call that a disaster? What about my six on the 10th!'

28 July 2000

'Is there a prize for nearest the bin?'

18 August 2000

'Still no sign of intelligence, then?'

25 August 2000

'I have heard about carrying your partner, but this is ridiculous.'

1 September 2000

'It makes your eyes water when he uses his driver!'

15 September 2000

'Father, have you forgotten? We've a match at nine o'clock.'

29 September 2000

'I now pronounce you man and wife – you may kiss the old bag.'

6 October 2000

'I only said "I'd like to get my hands on that
Big Bertha in the Pro shop".'

13 October 2000

'And they say we're slow! It took him 55 years
to get out of that bunker!'

3 November 2000

'I think she just offered him a gimme.'

17 November 2000

'Don't be long with her, there's a foursome coming up behind.'

24 November 2000

'Tell Mr Van de Velde his five minutes are up
and we're playing through.'

1 December 2000

'Congratulations, you've just won nearest the pin.'

15 December 2000

'You're lucky. The last person to upset him couldn't
sit down for a month.'

22 December 2000

'Hamish – shall I use a new teabag as it's nearly Christmas?'

29 December 2000

'Stupid men. I told them not to drink and drive.'

19 January 2001

'Try putting a little less backspin on them, Beryl!'

26 January 2001

'He'll be sorry on the back nine – I gave him an enema this morning!'

9 February 2001

'After my hole-in-one, can you make sure the bar's empty?'

16 February 2001

'If it wasn't for sweet Lolita here, I'd go completely out of my mind.'

23 February 2001

'It's great, but when he gets the wrong frequency
my garage doors open.'

2 March 2001

'Get going! My turn for "a round with Alice".'

9 March 2001

'If HE says wearing a skirt allows him to play from the ladies'
tee, he can play from the ladies' tee!'

16 March 2001

'Could I have the flag out, please?'

6 April 2001

'I bet he won't forget to rake the bunker again.'

13 April 2001

'I think he should have let the vicar play through.'

4 May 2001

'Well, there's Fred's ball – but where's Fred?'

8 June 2001

'No, I'm Rolf with an "R".'

15 June 2001

'Keep your heads down, lads – this one could go anywhere!'

21 June 2001

'Ethel works in the sales and marketing department.'

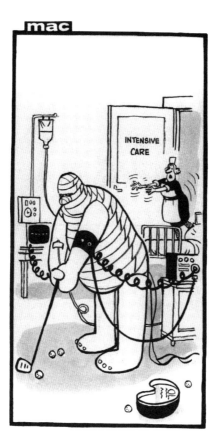

6 July 2001

'Mr Jones, put those gallstones back in the jar at once!'

13 July 2001

'It's a Titleist 3, missus, with two red dots.'

27 July 2001

'How lucky can you get? A hole-in-one on the first and now this.'

10 August 2001

'She was his teacher at High School.'

31 August 2001

'Take me to your leaderboard.'

7 September 2001

'Oi! We're not that slow!'

14 September 2001

'Well I don't know why he can't go behind a bush like the rest of us.'

21 September 2001

'OK, OK, Mavis, I'll mow the lawn this afternoon.'

28 September 2001

'Oh, look, it's Nick Fido.'

12 October 2001

'Funny – five pints ago I didn't fancy him at all.'

19 October 2001

'Great round, Sid! Birdie, eagle, albatross –
and now going for a seagull!'

2 November 2001

'Now we know what happened to Woosie's
caddie and the extra club.'

9 November 2001

'She only asked the men's fourball in front
if they would like to let us through!'

16 November 2001

'Oi! Take these or I'll call the police!'

23 November 2001

'Fancy a two-ball?'

30 November 2001

'I think they're working – Bill's down to 45 holes a week!'

4 January 2002

'Do you think I put too much brandy in the pudding?'

1 February 2002

'Would now be a good time to let the fourball behind play through?'

16 February 2002

'I think 2ft to the right. You got any thoughts, Doreen?'

15 March 2002

'Doesn't he know the trolley ban is lifted?'

22 March 2002

'Ethel, are you giving me this putt or not?'

5 April 2002

'When I said "a good drive across the water should do it",
I didn't mean in this thing, you idiot.'

12 April 2002

'I don't think you are allowed to put a tee peg there.'

26 April 2002

'Relax, relax – all the warders play golf today.'

3 May 2002

'Can you tell me where the visitors' changing-room is?'

24 May 2002

'No, it's not a new head cover.'

14 June 2002

'I'm just hoping he is a vegetarian.'

21 June 2002

'How do you say "I love you" in Arabic?'

28 June 2002

'Tom said his nearest point of relief was in the car park!'

19 July 2002

'You should see it in the winter –
there was one day we couldn't play at all!'

23 August 2002

'Quick march. When they said Montgomerie,
I bet you lot thought it was going to be Colin.'

30 August 2002

'And lastly, don't forget to repair your pitch mark!'

6 September 2002

'I get sick of hanging about watching you enjoying yourself.'

20 September 2002

'Wonderful, but will they allow designer genes in the clubhouse?'

27 September 2002

'He's just got the bar bill for his hole-in-one.'

18 October 2002

'He said I should remember him for what he'd done with his life.'

1 November 2002

'Coincidentally, her husband's small and bald too!'

8 November 2002

'As I was saying, Peter and Thelma came round for dinner last night.'

22 November 2002

'I understand his dear departed was an usherette.'

6 December 2002

'Only one lump please, Bob.'

13 December 2002

'I wonder what the fellow who nicked
the lake balls is doing for a living now?'

24 January 2003

'Look, if you're that desperate, do like the male
members do – go into the bushes.'

31 January 2003

'The balls these days cost an arm and a...'

7 February 2003

'There's a mouse at the door –
wants to know if you want to buy some golf balls.'

14 February 2003

'Well, you can see what his handicap is!'

21 February 2003

'Leave it on, Fred, it'll help keep your head still.'

7 March 2003

'It's apparent from here, dear, they don't check
players' equipment as carefully as they should!'

21 March 2003

'I think I've got just the man to clear that minefield.'

28 March 2003

'The good news is – it's a free drop from tractor tracks!'

4 April 2003

'Well, it's got to be easier than entering that blasted caption competition in the *Mail*!'

11 April 2003

'Looks like you've got another good 'un there, Mrs Rooney.'

18 April 2003

'Do stop moaning, Madge. It's only once a year.'

2 May 2003

'There he goes. I keep warning him about
practising his swing in the window box.'

9 May 2003

'He says he was only trying to help you capture the
gaping void at the centre of our futile existence.'

16 May 2003

'I told him to drop in when he'd finished playing golf'

23 May 2003

'Just another few feet and they can put the sand in, Betty.'

6 June 2003

'Sorry, Lord, this fellow's so slow I'm going to be late for the service.'

20 June 2003

'It was a present from his mother-in-law.'

18 July 2003

'Well, I carried *him* for nine months.'

1 August 2003

'Why is he looking in the lake? My ball's right here.'

8 August 2003

'Just a few more and we'll start the lesson.'

15 August 2003

'Tell your missus we're only playing for a fiver.'

22 August 2003

'Dammit, Ethel! How many more balls are you going to lose?'

29 August 2003

'A spot of luck the ship sinking here.
Do you think the wives got off OK?'

12 September 2003

'That's enough putting. Let's move on to the driving section.'

19 September 2003

'I just used a couple of cans of starch.'

25 September 2003

'Hey, you're standing on the greenkeeper.'

3 October 2003

'At last, thank God you're here. It's a brand new
Pro VI Number Two with two black dots!'

10 October 2003

'You want a hole-in-one? OK, which knee?'

17 October 2003

'Shall we concede the match, Alf, and pay him the pound?'

7 November 2003

'Tended, please!'

14 November 2003

'I think he's more interested in christening those new golf clubs.'

21 November 2003

'No wonder it's stroke index one.'

28 November 2003

'Your flies are undone!'

19 December 2003

'I think they heard us saying we'd like to get rid of our old bags.'

2 January 2004

'Forget Wilson, think Dyson.'

9 January 2004

'The committee shouldn't have told him to
make the greens easier to read.'

23 January 2004

'You always said you wanted a trophy wife.'

30 January 2004

'Whoopee! I've just been drawn with Bing Crosby,
Bob Hope and Bobby Jones in the fourball.'

27 February 2004

'There's a good dog, now go and fetch Daddy's paint brush.'

5 March 2004

'That's either his technologically advanced golf ball or
Ronnie Corbett is lost in the rough again!'

12 March 2004

'Port, starboard, port, port!'

19 March 2004

'Quite a unique property, golf driving
range to front, army firing range to rear.'

2 April 2004

'The Pro told him to stand further away from the ball.'

9 April 2004

'You're lucky, last time he did it he only sent me a text.'

16 April 2004

'When you started trying to get out of this
bunker, it was only 2ft deep.'

23 April 2004

'They should never have voted Ken Livingstone on to the committee.'

30 April 2004

'I'm now nine up after nine. What did you wish for?'

7 May 2004

'Seems like a lot of trouble just to keep his toupee on.'

14 May 2004

'Apparently it's his mother's fault he missed.'

21 May 2004

'You'll have to speed up a bit, Charlie, we're due to tee off in an hour.'

4 June 2004

'When did Ray Reardon chuck the snooker, then?'

25 June 2004

'I'll go once you get everybody off the fairway!'

9 July 2004

'Oops, you've left yourself a nasty 29,035 ft uphiller.'

23 July 2004

'So, you're cremating your granny? Well, now you've both been fired!'

30 July 2004

'Hang on, skipper, we're just having yonder tree uprooted!'

13 August 2004

'If I was you, I would declare the ball lost.'

3 September 2004

'I would much prefer high tea at the Ritz.'

10 September 2004

'I see old Bill is still pulling your leg.'

17 September 2004

'Just imagine Sue Barker on *A Question of Sport*
– what happened next?'

1 October 2004

'I think we'll name your child Chip, Mrs Beck.'

22 October 2004

'He told the wife he was only popping out for a paper.'

12 November 2004

'I didn't think Trinny and Susannah would play.'

19 November 2004

'Yoo hoo! You've left your putter behind!'

10 December 2004

'His partner's a lepidopterist, you know.'

24 December 2004

'That's three birdies, Fred – first an eagle,
then an albatross and now a turkey!'

14 January 2005

'Make any offer under a pound, mate, and she's yours.'

21 January 2005

'Luvverly stance, 'Arry, but mind you don't 'it them elephants!'

28 January 2005

'Drop the flag, that's what these nutters aim for!'

4 March 2005

'No, he's not mine, but he'll keep the cats off my lawn!'

11 March 2005

'Hello, Frank, I can make it after all. I've just
dropped the wife off, see you in half an hour!'

18 March 2005

'You haven't seen anything yet.
She will put disinfectant down the hole in a minute.'

1 April 2005

'No, no! When I said "Take the old bag", I didn't mean that one.'

6 May 2005

'Out of the two of 'em I'd say Fred's missus has got the better grip.'

13 May 2005

'You were right, Bert. It *is* your wife and mistress ... mine too!'

20 May 2005

'Now as soon as I shout "Fore", ignite and stand back.'

27 May 2005

'I need to go to the loo!'

3 June 2005

'That's a nuisance. I really wanted a new trolley!'

10 June 2005

'He told me it was payback time for when I taught him maths.'

24 June 2005

'Wake up! You've had me up and down by my ears all night.'

8 July 2005

'It was fate – turns out we're both hookers.'

15 July 2005

'One day his golf umbrella will fail to open properly.'

26 August 2005

'My God! You're gonna win the Mac Golf Cartoon competition.'

2 September 2005

'Try shaking a golf ball down your trouser leg now.'

9 September 2005

'Shout when you want the brake off.'

23 September 2005

'When I said "play through", I didn't mean literally.'

30 September 2005

'I don't think that Vindaloo agreed with Harry.'

14 October 2005

'Any chance of you missing the cut?'

21 October 2005

'I told you to putt left, right, left-left, right on that hole!'

28 October 2005

'You know, you could just take the drop-shot.'

4 November 2005

'That was the bloke you always hear on TV shouting "In the hole".'

11 November 2005

'God works in mysterious fairways!'

3 February 2006

'Turn it off, turn it off, my zip's undone!'

3 March 2006

'Eight-footers don't frighten me!'

10 March 2006

'Fred, forget the emotion, here's the emulsion!'

4 August 2006

'It's happy hour in the clubhouse!'

11 August 2006

'For the first time in 30 years, me and the wife are both happy!'

CAPTION COMPETITION WINNERS

1 July 1999	A.J. Hart, Ormesby, Middlesbrough
15 July 1999	W.T. Hopwood, Newton, Powys
5 August 1999	C. Brinton, Gurnard, Isle of Wight
20 August 1999	Ian Hunter, Leigh, Lancashire
2 September 1999	J.T. Rudd, Washington, Tyne & Wear
9 September 1999	M. Brand, Wellingborough, Northamptonshire
17 September 1999	Keith Marriner, Hinckley, Leicestershire
23 September 1999	J.H. White, Axminster, Devon
30 September 1999	J. Wright, Attenborough, Nottinghamshire
7 October 1999	Mrs and Mrs G.W. James, Sheffield
21 October 1999	T. Barnes, Accrington, Lancashire
28 October 1999	Ray Hughes, Pontyclun, Mid Glamorgan, Wales
11 November 1999	R. Bowman, Colchester, Essex
18 November 1999	Bob Bates, Skegness, Lincolnshire
10 December 1999	Alan Campbell, Northampton
21 January 2000	E. Rhead, Wrightington, Wigan
4 February 2000	David Phillips, Porthcawl, South Wales
11 February 2000	Mike Reeve, Hornchurch, Essex
17 March 2000	Mrs L. Bacchus, Cowes, Isle of Wight
31 March 2000	H. Crawford, Bexleyheath
21 April 2000	L. Slaughter, Bexhill-on-Sea, Sussex
28 April 2000	Mrs Pat Mason, Sandbach, Cheshire
5 May 2000	P.J. Burns, Portishead, Bristol
12 May 2000	John A. Woodward, Stondon Massey, Brentwood, Essex
19 May 2000	Maggie Hutchinson, Dolgellau, Gwynedd, Wales
26 May 2000	C. Reynolds, Cowplain, Hampshire
2 June 2000	J. Touzel, Broadstairs, Kent
9 June 2000	M. Goodwin, Potters Bar, Hertfordshire
23 June 2000	K. Frost, Worthing, Sussex
14 July 2000	H.J. Blackmore, Maesteg, Glamorganshire, Wales
21 July 2000	Brian Morris, Rye, Sussex
28 July 2000	A. Sayburn, Cleveleys, Blackpool
18 August 2000	Linda McDonnell, Sevenoaks, Kent
25 August 2000	Austin Stewart, Birkenhead
1 September 2000	Dinas Cross, Newport, Pembrokeshire
15 September 2000	J. Arthur, Colchester, Essex
29 September 2000	S. Warrilow, Newport
6 October 2000	E. Wells, Midhurst, Surrey
13 October 2000	K. Ramsden, Shipley, West Yorkshire
3 November 2000	D. West, Swadlincote, Derbyshire
17 November 2000	Mrs E. Allan, Purley, Surrey
24 November 2000	P. Rothwell, Downley, High Wycombe, Buckinghamshire
1 December 2000	J. Keates, Chichester, West Sussex
15 December 2000	Andrew Griffiths, Kestrel Garth, Morley, Leeds
22 December 2000	D.Mason, Sandbach, Cheshire
29 December 2000	P. Emberton, Shropshire

19 January 2001	A.J. Edwards, Luton, Bedfordshire
26 January 2001	Tony Lewis, Sidcup, Kent
9 February 2001	I. Taylor, Barlborough, Chesterfield, Derbyshire
16 February 2001	John Brooker, Hove, East Sussex
23 February 2001	Kevin Charles, Minster-on-Sea, Kent
2 March 2001	R. Ash, Windsor, Berkshire
9 March 2001	A. Matthews, Manchester
16 March 2001	D. Pimm, Powys, Wales
6 April 2001	W. Brooks, Woodley, Berkshire
13 April 2001	A.D. Gray, Great Harwood, Lancashire
4 May 2001	Colin Rush, Stowmarket, Suffolk
8 June 2001	R. Edmonds, Welwyn, Hertfordshire
15 June 2001	K. Newton, Rochford, Essex
21 June 2001	Mike Frankish, Stamford, Lincolnshire
6 July 2001	R. Burridge, Exeter, Devon
13 July 2001	Mrs A. Boyd, Prestwick, Scotland
27 July 2001	F. Bartram, Brentwood, Essex
10 August 2001	Michael McKeown, Bognor Regis, West Sussex
31 August 2001	Bill Jackson, Edinburgh
7 September 2001	P.A. Rees, Rhondda Cynon Taff, Wales
14 September 2001	T.F. Taylor, Washington, Tyne & Wear
21 September 2001	R. Monk, Peterborough
28 September 2001	P. Messenger, Bristol
12 October 2001	Bob Quirk, Birkenhead
19 October 2001	F.Dugdale, Nelson, Lancashire
2 November 2001	J. Stevenson, Paignton, Devonshire
9 November 2001	Mrs June Warne, Scunthorpe
16 November 2001	Mrs J.Holton, Milton Keynes
23 November 2001	Trevor Buckley, Lytham St Annes, Lancashire
30 November 2001	Mark Dougall, Kircaldy, Fife
4 January 2002	B. Evans, Ebbw Vale, Gwent, Wales
1 February 2002	J. Keates, Chichester, West Sussex
16 February 2002	Ian Taylor, Chesterfield, Derbyshire
15 March 2002	C.Hibbert, Windsor, Berkshire
22 March 2002	Alex Caldwell, Huddersfield
5 April 2002	A.F. Jenkins, Stone Cross, Pevensey, East Sussex
12 April 2002	Derek Darby, Aylesford, Kent
26 April 2002	Bill Lawrence, Maesycummer, Mid Glamorgan, Wales
3 May 2002	Mike O'Mara, Widnes, Cheshire
24 May 2002	Mark Hughes, Blackley, Manchester
14 June 2002	Andrew Whittaker, Rossendale, Lancashire
21 June 2002	Edd Coombes, Leigh-on-Sea, Essex
28 June 2002	Julie McFee, Carlisle
19 July 2002	Doug Hutchison, Arbroath, Scotland
23 August 2002	Louis Barratt, Clacton, Essex
30 August 2002	R.I. McNeal, Middlesbrough
6 September 2002	Alan Robson, Dunston, Tyne & Wear
20 September 2002	Bob Foggo, High Wycombe, Buckinghamshire
27 September 2002	J.Keates, Chichester, Sussex
18 October 2002	Ian Mann, Rosehill Marple, Stockport
1 November 2002	John Turner, Hibaldstow, Brigg, North Lincolnshire
8 November 2002	Don Wells, Fleet, Hampshire
22 November 2002	Jack Jackson, West Heath, Birmingham

Date	Name
6 December 2002	Michael Smallcombe, Esher, Surrey
13 December 2002	R.E. Finney, Woodford Green, Essex
24 January 2003	Anthony Parker, New Mills, High Peak
7 February 2003	Roy Harrison, Lathom, Lancashire
14 February 2003	G. Winslade, Weymouth, Dorset
21 February 2003	Greg Collis, Rossendale, Lancashire
7 March 2003	Alan Morton, Wymondham, Norfolk
21 March 2003	Andrew Connor, Great Barr, Birmingham
28 March 2003	P. Rowley, Alsager, Cheshire
4 April 2003	D. Ford, Woodford Green, Essex
11 April 2003	E. Smyth, Pinner, Middlesex
18 April 2003	R.J. Barker, Chippenham
2 May 2003	Gordon Wood, Bishop's Stortford, Hertfordshire
9 May 2003	Archie Foster, Sheffield
16 May 2003	A. Robson, Gateshead, Tyne & Wear
23 May 2003	R. Ward, Ludlow, Shropshire
6 June 2003	Maurice Bonner, Bordon, Hampshire
20 June 2003	Paula Angell, Cholesbury, Tring, Hertfordshire
18 July 2003	Mrs M. Mason, Penridge, Staffordshire
1 August 2003	Steven Worthy, Hilton
8 August 2003	W. Crompton, Wendover, Buckinghamshire
15 August 2003	Terry Collins, Chingford, Essex
22 August 2003	W. Smith, Ranskill, Nottinghamshire
29 August 2003	K. Richardson, Wednesbury, West Midlands
12 September 2003	Barry Sheffield, Batley
19 September 2003	Paul Wade, Hailsham, East Sussex
25 September 2003	David Walker, Aberdeen
3 October 2003	B. Potter
10 October 2003	D. Reid, Perth
17 October 2003	John Halsall Southport, Merseyside
7 November 2003	Garry Clark, Eastbourne, East Sussex
14 November 2003	Jonathan Eddy, Torpoint, Cornwall
21 November 2003	Tony Bettles, Longfield, Kent
28 November 2003	John Lisk, Ifold, West Sussex
19 December 2003	Robin Wickham, Norwich
2 January 2004	Derek Newbold, Paignton, South Devon
9 January 2004	Robert Armstrong, Cramlington, Northumberland
23 January 2004	Louise Collins, Isleworth
30 January 2004	Francis Dugdale, Nelson, Lancashire
27 February 2004	H. Scott, Baldock, Hertfordshire
5 March 2004	M. Keenan, Kilmarnock, Scotland
12 March 2004	David Nicholas, Rugby
19 March 2004	Peter Dallas, Neilston, Glasgow
2 April 2004	Lynne Evans, Huddersfield
9 April 2004	Mark Beach, Old Stratford, Milton Keynes
16 April 2004	Mrs J. Maclean, Hesket Newmarket, Cumbria
23 April 2004	Steve Eastwood, Bulwell, Nottinghamshire
30 April 2004	Nigel Hanna, West Hunsbury, Northampton
7 May 2004	Michael Page, Farnborough, Hampshire
14 May 2004	Jay Maclean, Hesket Newmarket, Cumbria
21 May 2004	Stephen Loten, Fleet, Hampshire
4 June 2004	Charles Ferguson, Glasgow
25 June 2004	Jim Hastings, Cardiff

9 July 2004	Richard Dyson, Sheffield
23 July 2004	Phil Cook, Cheltenham, Gloucestershire
30 July 2004	Bryan Owram, Esholt, West Yorkshire
13 August 2004	Kenneth Roberts, Dover, Kent
3 September 2004	Nick Naylor, Burnham, Buckinghamshire
10 September 2004	David Walsh, Burnley, Lancashire
17 September 2004	C. Davies, Hough, near Crewe
1 October 2004	W. Smith, Frinton-on-Sea, Essex
22 October 2004	George McGrade, Glasgow
12 November 2004	Barry Burton, Fareham, Hampshire
19 November 2004	Mrs Betty Tosdevin, Gosport, Hampshire
10 December 2004	J. Chester-Bristow, Rotherham
24 December 2004	John Morris, Blackpool
14 January 2005	George James, Weston Coyney, Staffordshire
21 January 2005	W. Littlewood, Alton, Hampshire
28 January 2005	S. Corcoran, Leigh, Lancashire
4 March 2005	Bryan Owram, Esholt, West Yorkshire
11 March 2005	Ricky Moonan, Knightswood, Glasgow
18 March 2005	Mrs L. Malt, King's Lynn, Norfolk
1 April 2005	Bryan Owram, Esholt, West Yorkshire
6 May 2005	E.Masters, London
13 May 2005	Ian McLaren, Edinburgh
20 May 2005	C. Manisier, Brentwood, Essex
27 May 2005	G.Brown, Leicester
3 June 2005	Paul Wood, Derby
10 June 2005	Ian Mowat, Morley, Leeds
24 June 2005	M. Smallcombe, Esher, Surrey
8 July 2005	Robert Emmet Logan, London
15 July 2005	M. O'Mara, Widnes, Cheshire
26 August 2005	Richard Jones, Farncombe, Surrey
2 September 2005	Mike Bridgeman, Devizes, Wiltshire
9 September 2005	C. Barrett, Seaford, Sussex
23 September 2005	Colin Laban, Mexborough, South Yorkshire
30 September 2005	Tricia McCunnell, Hull
14 October 2005	Douglas Peachey, Langland, Swansea
21 October 2005	Stan Briggs, Banstead, Surrey
4 November 2005	Ken Lane, Bournemouth
11 November 2005	Keith Rowlands, Shirenewton, Chepstow
3 February 2006	David Trowe, Quorn, Leicestershire
3 March 2006	Ron Sands, Cleethorpes
10 March 2006	Raymond Bowden, St Austell, Cornwall
4 August 2006	James Peel, Basingstoke, Hampshire
11 August 2006	Connor Milligan, Kilmarnock, Scotland